MONTY AND THE POMPSTERS

Written and illustrated

by Gabriela E. Stone

Monty the monster

lived on a grey hill.

At the top of the summit,

he could feel the wind's chill.

The trees there, were dark,

so was the river.

With black little fishes

that couldn't get bigger

The foot of the hill,

was surrounded with thorns.

He never went down there.

He was cold and alone.

Down in the valley,

on the green and soft ground,

lived a family of creatures

all fluffy and round.

One day, whilst out walking

high up on his hill,

Monty tripped over.

He took quite a spill.

He rolled from the summit.

He rolled round and round

and into the valley

of the strange little crowd.

He flattened the thorns there,

he flattened them good,

as into the valley

sun started to flood.

The Pompsters were frightened;

they were bouncing around,

as they looked down at Monty

lying flat on the ground.

Who are you stranger?

You've had quite a spill

Are you the creature,

who lives on the hill?

Monty then grunted,

and leapt to his feet.

"I live on the hill,

I'm glad we could meet".

"Up on the hill",

He explained a bit dazed,

"It's dark in the nights

and grey in the days".

It's mostly cloudy

and when the night falls

the cricket chirps loudly

and the lonely wolf calls"

The colourful Pompsters

then stood by the trees

as their mighty chief leader

came forward and sneezed.

"It's different in here,

unlike there on the heights.

The weather is warm

and we've got scenic sights".

"If you stay with us now,

we can have fun and play.

Before you return

at the end of the day".

Monty was happy

With the new friends he'd found.

They skipped with a rope

and scared moles in the ground.

They played hide and seek

and chased a white bunny.

They rolled in the ditch

until they got muddy.

Monty was happy

but he had a long way,

to climb up the hill

at the end of the day.

"I will see you tomorrow",

He waved at them smiling.

As up the hill,

He then started climbing

"Let us come with you.

It will be a delight,

to visit your home

and stay overnight".

So Monty said;

"Sure, the day is not done.

We still have time,

to have lots more fun".

At the top of the summit,

they sang like a choir.

Roasting marshmallows

Sitting by the fire.

Monty and the Pompsters

Are now best of friends

and so, this is how

our little story ends.